The U.S. Constitution
& Bill of
Rights

Essential Events

THE U.S. CONSTITUTION
R & BILL OF RIGHTS

BY CHARLES E. PEDERSON

Content Consultant
Peter J. Smith
Professor, George Washington University Law School

ABDO
Publishing Company

CREDITS

Published by ABDO Publishing Company, 8000 West 78th Street, Edina, Minnesota 55439. Copyright © 2010 by Abdo Consulting Group, Inc. International copyrights reserved in all countries. No part of this book may be reproduced in any form without written permission from the publisher. The Essential Library™ is a trademark and logo of ABDO Publishing Company.

Printed in the United States of America,
North Mankato, Minnesota
102009
012010

 PRINTED ON RECYCLED PAPER

Editor: Amy Van Zee
Copy Editor: Paula Lewis
Interior Design and Production: Becky Daum
Cover Design: Becky Daum

Library of Congress Cataloging-in-Publication Data
Pederson, Charles E.
   The U.S. Constitution & Bill of Rights / Charles E. Pederson.
      p. cm. — (Essential events)
   Includes bibliographical references and index.
   ISBN 978-1-60453-948-6
   1. United States. Constitution—Juvenile literature. 2. United States—Politics and government—1775-1783—Juvenile literature. 3. United States—Politics and government—1783-1789—Juvenile literature. I. Title. II. Title: The U.S. Constitution and Bill of Rights.
   E303.P43 2010
   342.7302—dc22

                           2009031149

The U.S. Constitution & Bill of Rights

TABLE OF CONTENTS

Chapter 1	Those Arguing Patriots	6
Chapter 2	What Came Before	14
Chapter 3	Chaos and Confusion	24
Chapter 4	Convention Attendees	34
Chapter 5	The Convention Begins	42
Chapter 6	Deadlocks	52
Chapter 7	The Convention Ends	62
Chapter 8	Ratification	72
Chapter 9	The Bill of Rights	82
Timeline		96
Essential Facts		100
Additional Resources		102
Glossary		104
Source Notes		106
Index		109
About the Author		112

The Constitutional Convention met in Philadelphia, Pennsylvania, in 1787.

THOSE ARGUING PATRIOTS

During the summer of 1787, a small group of men were sweltering in Philadelphia, Pennsylvania. Some wore long wool coats. Some wore white powdered wigs made of horsehair. These merchants, lawyers, politicians, and planters were

members of the Constitutional
Convention, and they had been
arguing for many weeks. They were
trying to make a nation out of 13
individual states, and it was not easy.
Each state had its own interests. Each
state was proud of its self-rule. None
of the states wanted to give up power.

A Declaration and a War

In late 1774, another group of
men had assembled in Philadelphia
for the First Continental Congress
with the purpose of declaring the
colonies' rights. Some of those men
were present in Philadelphia for the
1787 Constitutional Convention.
Some were famous, such as Benjamin Franklin.
Others were not as famous, such as Roger Sherman
and Robert Morris. Sherman was a politician in
his home state of Connecticut. Morris had been
a financier during the Revolutionary War, raising
money for George Washington's army.

In 1775, the colonies had gone to war against
Britain. They wanted to separate from that empire

Philadelphia Facts

William Penn, a member
of the Quaker religious
group, had founded Philadelphia around 1682. By
the 1780s, Philadelphia
had grown considerably.
African-American slaves
and ex-slaves, German-speaking farmers, and
native tribespeople from
the nearby Delaware
nation walked the streets.
Those streets were not
always clean. Away from
the wealthier sections,
one could see garbage and
even dead animals lying
in the streets. There were
no underground sewers or
indoor bathrooms. People
used chamber pots. They
sometimes emptied the
pots onto the streets outside their homes.

and its ruler, King George III. The delegates to the
Second Continental Congress wrote a document
outlining their reasons for rejecting British rule.
But they also argued as they worked toward a decision
about the principles upon which their new nation
would be founded. Finally, on July 4, 1776, the men
signed an important document—the Declaration of
Independence. This laid out a blueprint for a new
country, one that did not have a king. It was meant
to be a country founded on equality and respect for
people's rights.

The men had put themselves at great risk by
holding such a meeting. If the British army had
captured them, they would have been hanged as
traitors. Although the war had started before the
declaration was signed, this document made their
complaints official.

After eight years, the colonies won the
Revolutionary War (1775–1783) against Britain.
The victory astounded the world. At that time, the
British army was the most powerful in the world.
In contrast, the small colonial armies were poorly
paid and poorly armed. Many of these men were
not full-time soldiers. They were members of states'
militias—groups of part-time soldiers who trained

British troops surrendered at Yorktown in 1781.

to fight in emergencies. These farmers, innkeepers, doctors, and blacksmiths were angry at the way the king treated them and their lack of representation in the British parliament. Their passion led them to victory.

The last big battle of the Revolutionary War was fought at Yorktown, Virginia, in 1781. George Washington led the Continental army. British General Charles Cornwallis and his army were trapped between Washington's army and the Chesapeake Bay. The British surrendered, and the two parties signed a treaty in 1783.

UNITING THE STATES

In 1783, there were 13 former British colonies in North America. Each colony had its own unique history. Their forms of government were similar in some ways and different in others. During the war, the colonies had worked together to fight Britain. After the war, they decided to continue to work together as much as possible. However, none of the states, as the colonies called them, wanted to give up any power. They had argued about signing the Declaration of Independence. They still had difficulties in compromising.

During the Constitutional Convention of 1787, the men argued about the states' relative power. Should the larger states have more power? They argued about how to make a new Congress. How many representatives should each state have? They argued about how to choose a president. Should each citizen have one vote? Should the states' lawmakers choose? They argued about slavery. Should it be allowed? If so, how long should it continue? Should it be legal in any new states that might be created? If slavery should not be allowed, how and when should it end? The group argued about taxation. Should taxes be based on population numbers? If so, how much should slaves count? They argued about how to keep the new government from becoming too strong and which powers it should have. They argued about which rights the states should keep.

These were not easy questions to answer. Each state's representative had his own ideas. There were times when it seemed the United States would fall apart as a nation. The predictions of

Benjamin Franklin's Modern Philadelphia

At the time of the Constitutional Convention, Philadelphia was quite an advanced city, thanks, in large part, to Benjamin Franklin's contributions. Franklin had traveled overseas and learned from other cultures. Some of the things he saw in other countries became the models for his later inventions. He never patented his inventions. Instead, he wanted them to be available without cost to everyone.

Franklin was not only known for his inventions; he believed in community service. Franklin organized the Pennsylvania state militia. In 1731, he founded the first library in North America. Members contributed money to buy books and then could use the books for free. The Library Company of Philadelphia still exists.

Fires were a constant danger in Philadelphia and in other large cities. So in 1736, Franklin organized a fire department to help respond to fire emergencies. Franklin also wanted the streets of Philadelphia to be safer after dark and helped get street lamps installed. These and many more of Franklin's projects and ideas helped make Philadelphia a very modern city for its time.

Philadelphia State House

The Philadelphia State House, also called Independence Hall, was where the Declaration of Independence was adopted. It is also the site of the discussion, drafting, and signing of the U.S. Constitution. Construction of the building was started in 1732. It was paid for as money became available and was finished in 1753. Many historians consider Independence Hall to be the birthplace of the nation.

many European countries appeared to be coming true: this young country would argue so much that it would tear itself apart.

One of the delegates, Thomas Mifflin of Philadelphia, had made a speech during the Revolutionary War. He had said:

> *Let us not be bold in declarations and afterwards cold in action. Let not the patriotic feeling of today be forgotten tomorrow, nor have it said of Philadelphia that she passed noble resolutions, slept on them and afterwards neglected them.* [2]

Many of the delegates felt the ideas expressed in those words applied well to this convention. Would the men make noble speeches about a new country, only to let their differences keep it from happening? Would their patriotic feelings be surpassed by arguments? The delegates had good intentions to draft a constitution that would be the supreme law of their new country. That is, if the men could stop arguing long enough to actually write it.

Thomas Mifflin was a Pennsylvanian who fought in the Revolutionary War.

In this cartoon, each portion of the snake represents a colony. The cartoonist, Benjamin Franklin, believed unity was important.

WHAT CAME BEFORE

European nations in the mid–1700s were led by kings and emperors. Two empires at that time were Britain and France. These two enemy countries had been trying to expand their power for years.

TERRITORIAL CLAIMS
AND A REVOLUTION

Both Britain and France had made territorial claims in North America, which they considered the New World. At first, the two countries occupied and controlled different parts of the continent. However, by the mid-1700s, both nations began to expand into the same areas of central North America.

In an effort to protect their claims to the territory, the two countries fought the French and Indian War (1754–1763). While France tried to push the British from the area, the British tried to cut off France's supplies and make them give up the land. Finally, the British won the war, gaining all the territory that had belonged to France. This included the land between the Appalachian Mountains and the Mississippi River as well as most of Canada.

The French and Indian War

The French and Indian War was fought primarily between the French and the British. However, many American Indians fought for both sides during the war. The French who lived in Canada called it the *Guerre de la Conquete* (War of Conquest). They saw the British as conquerors who took away their land.

THE REVOLUTIONARY WAR

Along with the gained land, Britain incurred a large debt. Fighting against France had been very expensive. Now the British king and his lawmakers, the Parliament, needed to pay for the war. One idea was to make the 13 colonies pay the debt through taxes. Parliament passed a tax law and other laws that the colonists did not like. A slogan was adopted in the colonies: "No Taxation Without Representation."[1] The colonists had no one to represent them in Parliament. That meant Parliament could impose rules without hearing any opinions from the colonies.

Finally, the colonists revolted against the unfair taxes. They decided they could not be part of Britain anymore. In April 1775, the Revolutionary War began.

During the French and Indian War, the colonists had learned about guerilla fighting tactics from American Indians. In their bright red uniform jackets, the British army, often called the Redcoats, used a different approach. They stood in long lines of hundreds or thousands of men while they shot at their enemy. Because the British expected their enemy to do the same, they were unprepared for the guerilla warfare used by the colonists. The colonists fired from behind trees and hid in ambush as they fought Britain's larger and better-armed soldiers.

The Revolutionary War made the colonies realize something else important. Because each colony considered itself its own country, they were not united. Each had its own laws, customs, and history. But individually, no one colony could stand up against the might of the Redcoats.

Even before the war started, colonial leaders recognized the benefits of working together. They had formed Committees of Correspondence. These groups kept colonial leaders informed of what was happening throughout the colonies. When British soldiers killed a group of Boston citizens in 1770, soon all the other colonies knew about the event, later called the Boston Massacre.

Braddock's Defeat

The British army was considered the best in the world. But guerilla tactics defeated one large British force in 1755, during the French and Indian War.

British General Edward Braddock led approximately 1,200 soldiers against half that many French soldiers and their American Indian allies. The British soldiers were taught to stand in long lines and to fire at an enemy that did not move.

But the French and the American Indians did not stand still to fight. They fought from behind trees and used ambushes to attack the British.

The guerilla tactics worked. Many British soldiers were killed, while as few as 40 French soldiers and American Indians died.

British troops fired into a Boston crowd in 1770, during what was later called the Boston Massacre.

These correspondence groups led naturally to the next step. The colonial leaders decided to make a formal agreement. On November 15, 1777, they approved a document called the Articles of Confederation. They called it a "league of friendship" for their common defense.

All 13 colonies had to ratify, or approve, the document for it to take effect. The first to ratify it was Virginia, which did so on December 16, 1777. It took years for the other states to follow suit. Several states had claimed territory north of the Ohio River, where much of the French and Indian War had been fought. Until these claims were cleared up, several states would not agree to the Articles of Confederation. Maryland, for example, would not ratify the document until New York and Virginia gave up land claims in the Ohio River Valley. On March 1, 1781, three-and-a-half years after the ratification process had begun, Maryland was the last to ratify. When Maryland signed off, the Articles of Confederation took effect. The 13 separate states were now called the United States, but they were not united too closely.

FEATURES OF THE ARTICLES OF CONFEDERATION

The articles created a one-chamber lawmaking body, or legislature. That meant each state had one vote in the Congress. This Congress was generally called the Congress of the Confederation.

Under the articles, the states and the federal government were meant to share power. This central government, however, did not have many powers compared to the states. It could only declare war and manage foreign affairs. The states kept all of their other powers, such as printing money and trading with other states and countries.

The main problem for the Congress was it could not raise taxes. Without the power to tax on its own, the government had no money. It had to ask the states for money. Congress was given the job of regulating military affairs, but it had to ask the states for troops. And only reluctantly would the states send money or soldiers for the Continental army. The articles were flawed, but

The Boston Massacre

The Boston Massacre was one of the events that sparked the Revolutionary War. It occurred on March 5, 1770. Although five people were killed, many Boston citizens called the situation a massacre in order to draw attention to their cause.

British troops had been stationed in Boston since 1768, and the city's citizens were not pleased to have the troops occupying their streets. The situation was tense. On March 5, 1770, a riot began in the streets, and British officer Captain Preston assembled his men to control the crowd. As the crowd grew, the soldiers fired into the crowd. Three people were killed, and eight were wounded. Two of those who were wounded later died.

Captain Preston and his men were put on trial in Boston. John Adams, a lawyer, defended the British troops. The trials of Preston and his men were the longest in colonial history. In the end, Preston was found not guilty, as it could not be proven that he ordered his troops to fire. Two of his men, however, were found guilty. It was proven that they fired into the crowd.

changing any of them would be extremely difficult. In order to do so, all of the states had to agree.

During the Revolutionary War, it became clear how little power Congress had. The national army had few supplies and often did not have enough money to pay the soldiers. Lack of money caused a shortage of food for the army. Congress was supposed to run the war, but it was unable to unless the states provided money and men. The articles were too weak to provide for a national defense. George Washington and other military leaders noted this weakness. They later came to support a different kind of government.

The Articles of War

To govern the Continental army, the Congress adopted the Articles of War in 1775. These articles established the code of rules and conduct for army personnel based on a British model. They were used to administer discipline in the army. The Articles of War were kept in place until 1951, when they were replaced by the Uniform Code of Military Justice.

Despite the weaknesses, the Continental army continued to fight. Washington, its commanding general, was a highly respected and skilled leader. Also, guerilla warfare called for small, self-contained groups. They did not need as much help from a central government as a large, traditional army would.

Under Washington, the Continental army won the war. Washington was able to trap the last large army of Redcoats at Yorktown, Virginia. Unable to retreat, the British, under General Cornwallis, were forced to surrender on October 19, 1781. It was a bitter blow for the tough, experienced Redcoats. They found it difficult to understand how an army that seemed to be made up of ill-clad farmers and laborers could have defeated them.

The French and Indian War had led to war debts, which led to taxes. In turn, taxes led to a revolution, which led to independence for the 13 colonies. Where independence would lead the young nation was still unknown. ⌐

A folk artist's rendering of George Washington riding his horse

A newspaper announces the Treaty of Paris, which was signed in 1783.

CHAOS AND CONFUSION

After the surrender of the British at Yorktown, the British war effort in the states came to an end. In 1783, in Paris, France, the British signed the Treaty of Paris. This marked the end of the Revolutionary War. The treaty stated that all British troops would withdraw from areas west of the Appalachian Mountains and south of the Great Lakes. With the war ended, the Continental army disbanded. The soldiers were finally free to go home and resume their lives as farmers and small businessmen.

A Complicated Situation

The frailty of the Articles of Confederation was seen immediately. In lightly settled western areas, there were not enough soldiers to defend settlements and farms against American Indian raids. Also, despite the Treaty of Paris, not all British troops had left the area, as promised by the treaty. The militias were not strong enough to force the British out. Congress wanted to send more forces to strengthen the area. But the articles stated that Congress had to ask the states for money and men. The states were reluctant to send either.

The Articles of Confederation did not help pull the states together as a nation. Instead, they caused a system of chaos and confusion. The chaos was not only in military areas. The articles could not regulate business between states or negotiate their disputes, either.

The Brink of Disaster

Printing extra money proved to be a short-sighted solution to the economic problems facing the colonies. Soon, inflation was out of control. For example, "a pound of tea in some areas could be purchased for a tidy $100."[1]

Many citizens were unhappy with the situation. The states had run up large war debts. Some states tried to pay the debts by printing extra paper money, but this only lessened the value of the money. Other states tried to repay the debts by raising taxes, which their citizens were unable to pay. Farms and homes were foreclosed. Many people who could not repay their loans were held in debtor's prison until they could do so.

These poor economic conditions encouraged riots, but the central government did not have troops to stop the uprisings. Nor could the individual state militias handle the unrest. In addition, some veterans of the Revolutionary War had rioted. They had not received the bonuses that the federal government had promised them. Congress simply did not have the money to pay the men.

Because each state had its own currency, the states had to decide on exchange rates. An exchange rate is used to calculate how much one state's money can buy of another state's goods. The system was complicated, and economic chaos reigned.

For example, New York, which controlled the harbor in New York City, was charging neighboring states New Jersey and Connecticut high taxes on anything they brought into New York harbor. New Jersey and Connecticut began to meet to consider an armed attack on New York to gain access to the harbor.

Something needed to be done about the Articles of Confederation, but the problem was complicated. The states had fought hard to free themselves from British rule. Now they wanted to keep their independence, not only from Britain, but also from each other.

Exchange Rates

An exchange rate tells how much one country's currency, or money, is worth in terms of another country's money. It indicates how much of a country's product another can buy. For example, the United States uses dollars, and the United Kingdom uses pounds. If a U.S. citizen wants to purchase something from the United Kingdom, he or she would exchange dollars for pounds. The exchange rate determines this exchange. If one pound were worth $1.50, then something that costs three pounds would cost $4.50. Exchange rates are always changing. They reflect the demand for a country's currency at a given time.

European countries use a common currency known as the euro. It was created in 1999 to help neighboring European countries maintain a consistent exchange rate. The hope was to encourage trade between the nations. Also, the euro saves travelers in Europe from having to convert money every time they cross a border. As of 2009, 16 nations in Europe used the euro: Austria, Belgium, Finland, France, Germany, Greece, Ireland, Italy, Luxembourg, Malta, the Netherlands, Portugal, the Republic of Cyprus, Slovakia, Slovenia, and Spain.

Shays's Rebellion

As the states contemplated how to amend the articles, current events were lending a helping hand. In Massachusetts, Daniel Shays was angry. He had been a captain during the Revolutionary War. He had loyally and bravely fought at Bunker Hill in Boston. After the war, like thousands of other soldiers, he went home. He was tired of war and wanted only to return to his normal life. The British king no longer ruled him, and he was proud of helping achieve independence. He entered politics to serve his fellow farmers.

However, the Massachusetts legislature needed to pay off its war debts. It began to raise taxes. Soon, farmers and others were having a hard time making their payments. Their property was seized and sold to pay their debts. Some people were put in prison. Shays began to take part in demonstrations against the treatment of his friends and neighbors.

In late 1786, some of the farmers used armed force to shut down the courts of law. If the courts were closed, judges could not send anyone to prison. This stopped some of the imprisonments. In January 1787, Shays intended to permanently stop the poor treatment of farmers. He led an army of more than

A group of debt-ridden farmers led a revolt called Shays's Rebellion in 1786 and 1787.

1,000 men to Springfield, Massachusetts, where the government kept an arsenal of weapons and ammunition.

The Congress could not raise troops to stop the rebellion. Finally, the Massachusetts legislature raised militia troops. The problem was that the militiamen were not professional soldiers. They were farmers and small businessmen, much like Shays and his army. But by February 3, 1787, they had stopped the rebellion.

This success gave little comfort to the other states. Many feared something similar to Shays's Rebellion could happen in their own states. They did not want to wait for their state legislatures to gather a militia to put down riots and rebellions; they wanted a better way to assemble troops. Citizens began to ask themselves if a stronger central government was the answer.

There were other ongoing issues to consider as well. What if states broke into smaller regional confederations? They might even act on their own. If that happened, the states might be easy prey for Britain to reconquer. That might allow Spain, which ruled Florida and the coast of the Gulf of Mexico, to take over some of the states.

A DIFFERENT CALL TO ACTION

Even before Shays's Rebellion, a group of men were thinking of how to amend the Articles of Confederation

George Washington Reacts to Shays's Rebellion

George Washington was disgusted by Massachusetts' harsh reaction to Shays's Rebellion. He was disappointed that the government could not keep its own citizens' loyalty. He was equally concerned about how the international community would view the events. He said, "What a triumph for the advocates of despotism [dictatorship] to find that we are incapable of governing ourselves, and that systems founded on the basis of equal liberty are merely ideal & falacious [false]!"[2]

because of an important issue that arose between two states. In September 1786, representatives from Virginia and Maryland met at an estate overlooking the Potomac River. Parts of Virginia and Maryland bordered the river, which both states used for shipping. The representatives were working on agreements about how to share it.

During their discussion, the men called for a meeting in Annapolis, Maryland, with the leaders of all 13 states to review the Articles of Confederation. Hopes were high, but the turnout was disappointing. The only representatives who attended were from Delaware, New Jersey, New York, Pennsylvania, and Virginia.

Among those who were disappointed were Alexander Hamilton and James Madison. They wanted another meeting to be held. Again, the call went out for a new convention, this one to be held in Philadelphia on May 13, 1787. The purpose, as with the Annapolis Convention, was to revise the Articles of Confederation.

Invitees to Philadelphia included war hero and respected politician George Washington. After the Revolutionary War, some people were ready to make Washington a king because of his role in

The Cost of Doing Nothing

In 1786, James Madison was concerned about what would happen if nothing were done to stabilize the United States. He said, "If the present paroxysm of our affairs be totally neglected, our case may become desperate."[3]

winning the war. However, instead of savoring his power, Washington did something unexpected. He retired and went home to Mount Vernon, Virginia, to be a farmer again. Madison and Hamilton were eager to have Washington accept their invitation because of his unselfish actions. Washington's presence would encourage representatives from other states to attend.

Washington hesitated to attend because of worries about his reputation. Others hesitated because they worried it might be an illegal meeting—only Congress could propose changes to the articles. In the end, Congress approved the meeting but only as a means to revise the Articles of Confederation. Congress required the meeting delegates to report to Congress and the state legislatures whenever they proposed a change to an article. The states would then confirm the changes. Also, the delegates were to change as little as needed to make the articles function better. ⌐

George Washington writes at his home, Mount Vernon, Virginia.

James Madison played a very important role at the Constitutional Convention. He later became the fourth president of the United States.

CONVENTION ATTENDEES

In May 1787, James Madison arrived for the Philadelphia Convention, later called the Constitutional Convention. Few noticed that he had arrived. But he was to become an important part of the event. One of his roles was to take notes during the proceedings. Each day, he wrote down all the motions and suggestions of every delegate. Today, his many pages of notes provide a complete record of the convention, offering insight into what happened and why.

Madison himself was worried about the influence of the majority without another group or person to check its power. A large, powerful group could do as it pleased, regardless of the minority's interests. Madison wanted to avoid that situation by creating a stronger federal government.

A Tall Order

In early May, delegates began to arrive in Philadelphia. Seventy-four delegates had been invited. During the four months of the convention, 55 of these attended, but not all at the same time.

Men came from every state except Rhode Island. The government there was so afraid of losing its powers through a new constitution that it would not even participate. Rhode Island's leaders believed

William Pierce on James Madison

One convention delegate named William Pierce wrote down his impressions of the other delegates. About James Madison, he said, "What is very remarkable—every Person seems to acknowledge his greatness. . . . He always comes forward the best informed Man of any point in debate. . . . He is easy and unreserved among his acquaintance."[1]

the convention was a conspiracy to overthrow the established government.

Patrick Henry, an influential Virginia statesman, was invited but refused to attend. He disagreed with Madison's idea of a strong central government. Henry believed that strong state governments would best protect people's freedoms.

MERGING VIEWPOINTS

The citizens in the states came from many backgrounds. There were immigrants from Britain, Ireland, and Scotland. Germans, Dutch, and Africans from many nations also lived in the new nation. Religious groups included

Checks and Balances

People sometimes complain that nothing gets done in Washington DC. Some think the system is too complicated. Congress proposes a law, and it is discussed and debated. It must be passed by both houses of the Congress. Then, the president has the option to veto it or sign it.

There are other complicated procedures in Washington. The president cannot send soldiers to war unless Congress agrees. The president can suggest justices for the Supreme Court, but the Senate has to agree to the choices. These justices serve for life and can strike down laws that both Congress and the president have agreed on. This system is complicated, but it is so for a reason. This system of checks and balances was set in place so the people would not feel as if their government ruled as a king. When each of the three branches of government can check the others' power, no one branch can take control. The process may be slow, but the members of the Constitutional Convention believed it was the best way for the new government to be set up.

Anglicans, Catholics, Jews, Baptists, Quakers, Puritans, and many others. Because of this diversity, each state had developed its own laws, religious ideas, self-government, and economic systems—and they were protective of their unique societies.

The men who gathered had the task of merging many varying viewpoints into one document. Historically, governments controlled laws; this was to be a document of laws that would control the government. The 55 delegates were about to create a country governed by rules, not by a ruler.

They recognized that the nature of humans is to look after their own wants, and this nature causes conflict. They wished to create a government that would allow for conflict while providing solutions that did not resort to violence or personal whim. They envisioned a system that people would accept and respect, even when a decision went against them.

Ordinary Leaders

Many men who attended the Constitutional Convention are now famous to us. Although they were leaders in their home states, they also were ordinary people.

George Washington lost his teeth in his mid-twenties and had wooden dentures for much of his adult life. Benjamin Franklin enjoyed swimming.

Though many people admire these men, each had his faults. At the Constitutional Convention, Benjamin Franklin said, "When you assemble a number of men to have the advantage of their joint wisdom, you inevitably assemble with those men, all their prejudices, their passions, their errors of opinion, their local interests, and their selfish views."[2]

Benjamin Franklin was a famous inventor, politician, writer, and philosopher.

THE DELEGATES

The men who attended the Constitutional Convention are often called our Founding Fathers. They included George Washington, whose appearance was a great relief to Madison. Madison knew that Washington's presence gave the convention a sense of legitimacy, because of his military reputation and his well-known humility.

Benjamin Franklin was almost as well-known as Washington. He had been a printer, newspaper publisher, inventor, diplomat, and philosopher. He was 81 years old during the summer of the convention. It was difficult for him to walk, so he was carried around in a chair.

One of Franklin's fellow Pennsylvanians was James Wilson. Originally from Scotland, Wilson had signed the Declaration of Independence. He was a brilliant lawyer who had a deep grasp of constitutions and how they worked.

John Adams, a delegate from Massachusetts, also had signed the Declaration of Independence. He was a lawyer and had been a delegate to the first and second Continental Congress.

Alexander Hamilton had come from New York. During the Revolutionary War, he had been one of Washington's officers and a close confidant.

George Mason was one of the Virginia delegates. He had helped shape the Virginia Bill of Rights.

Thomas Jefferson

Thomas Jefferson had much influence during the Continental Congress. He drafted the initial Declaration of Independence.

But in 1787, when delegates were assembling for the Constitutional Convention, Jefferson was overseas. In 1784, Congress had sent Jefferson to France to discuss commerce treaties with the French, along with John Adams and Benjamin Franklin. During the Constitutional Convention, James Madison sent Jefferson a draft of the Constitution. Jefferson approved the draft, but urged Madison to include a bill of rights. Jefferson returned to the United States in 1789.

Thomas Jefferson, a Virginian who was unable to attend the convention, had praised him as being brilliant without being greedy.

John Dickinson arrived from Delaware. He was a shy, quiet man, but an excellent writer. He had earned the nickname "Penman of the Revolution," and he exercised great influence on the proceedings.

Gouverneur Morris, another Pennsylvanian, had helped create New York's state constitution and had a wide background in financial affairs. Morris gave 173 speeches during the convention, more than any other delegate. He is believed to have drafted many portions of the Constitution.

Benjamin Franklin was the oldest delegate. The youngest delegate was Jonathan Dayton of New Jersey, who was 26. The average age of the delegates was approximately 45. Most of the delegates had political backgrounds. Some were lawyers. Some had been legislators in their home states. Some had served in the Continental Congress. They were diverse men who represented diverse populations. They would play a crucial role in shaping the governing documents of the United States of America.

*Gouverneur Morris gave many speeches at the Constitutional Convention.
He favored a strong central government.*

A sketch of the Philadelphia State House

THE CONVENTION BEGINS

O n May 25, 1787, the delegates gathered at the Philadelphia State House. They had been granted permission by Congress to improve the Articles of Confederation. It is unclear whether they had the proper permission to create an entirely new government, although that is eventually what happened. The delegates sat in groups of threes and fours at small tables covered with green felt tablecloths. James Madison made sure to take a seat where he could see and hear everything that went on. He chose a spot just below a raised platform at the front of the room where the convention president would sit. Madison never missed a day, and he took notes on everything that was said and done.

Every night in his rented room, Madison reviewed his notes so he could remember everything that had happened during the day. He later said that making himself attend every session during that hot Philadelphia summer almost killed him. Due to his foresight and attention to detail, historians know almost everything that occurred during the convention.

FIRST ORDERS OF BUSINESS

The first order of business was to choose a president for the convention. Robert Morris of Pennsylvania nominated George Washington for that office.

William Jackson, Secretary

William Jackson of South Carolina was chosen as the convention secretary. He took notes on motions. He did not sign the Constitution as a delegate. Rather, he signed it at the end to certify that it was a true record of what the delegates had decided.

Washington was immediately chosen by unanimous vote as president. This was the only time the delegates would agree on anything unanimously. Washington accepted the position. At the same time, he apologized for being inexperienced. He asked the delegates to overlook any mistakes he might make. Then he took his place behind the table on the room's raised platform. For the next four months, he occupied that chair whenever the convention was in session.

The next order of business was to establish a rule of secrecy during discussions. No reporters were allowed in the room where the delegates were meeting. None of the delegates would speak about anything that went on in the sessions, even to family and friends. The intent was to allow the members to act and speak without worrying about their public images. They wanted to be able to discuss unpopular ideas. They wanted to be able to change their minds. They were also worried what might happen if word got out about what they were doing. Guards were posted at the doors to the State House to keep away the curious.

The secrecy was so strict that it made opponents of a new constitution suspicious of what was being

George Washington presided over debates at the Constitutional Convention.

decided. Thomas Jefferson, who was living in Paris at the time, was disappointed. He wrote, "I am sorry they began their deliberations by so abominable a precedent as that of tying up the tongues of their members."[1]

THE VIRGINIA PLAN

On Thursday, May 29, the third full day of the convention, Edmund Randolph, the governor of Virginia, rose to his feet. Randolph had plenty of experience in the Virginia legislature. He proposed the Virginia Plan, a plan that James Madison had helped devise. It contained a strong central government that could veto, or deny, the states' laws. The plan also contained a system whereby the national legislature would vote for the president. Because the legislators were elected by the people, the people would indirectly elect the president.

Also, the legislature would contain two branches. Members of the first branch would be chosen by the people. Members of the second branch would be selected from nominations by members of state legislatures. The number of delegates would be based on population. Larger states would have more representatives. This would give them more power in Congress.

The Virginia Plan had three challenges to overcome. First, such a strong central government was exactly what many of the delegates, especially those from smaller states, feared. The second problem was that Randolph was proposing eliminating the present government and replacing it with a completely new one. Not many favored such drastic measures. Finally, it was unclear whether the group had any legal right to create a new constitution. Their states had chosen them only to improve the Articles of Confederation.

The larger states liked the plan because it gave them more votes in the new Congress. The smaller states disliked the plan because it gave them less power. Unfortunately for these small states, they were outnumbered. Some delegates from smaller states had not yet arrived, and Rhode Island had no intention of sending anyone at all. This gave the larger states a majority of votes. The proposal made it to the floor. But it was not voted on immediately. Instead, ten days of passionate debate would follow.

The atmosphere at the convention was tense. One delegate described the situation by saying the convention was being held together by a hair. If the Virginia Plan was accepted, many of the smaller states might pull out of the United States altogether. Still, the plan seemed likely to pass.

While the Virginia Plan was being deliberated, some of the smaller states asked for the opportunity to present their own plan. This plan would favor the smaller states.

A New Jersey Plan and a British Plan

On Saturday, June 9, 1787, William Paterson proposed the New Jersey Plan. It was quite different from the Virginia Plan. Under the New Jersey Plan, each state would receive only one vote in Congress. This would be an advantage to small states because their votes would have the same weight as larger states. Additionally, this plan proposed a separate Supreme Court. The delegates from New Jersey, New York, and Delaware were in favor of this plan. After several days of debate,

The Virginia Plan Debate

The Virginia Plan was heavily debated with passionate speeches on both sides. Roger Sherman of Connecticut argued that the plan was no good because it disregarded the feelings of the general public. He believed people would be happier in small states than in large ones. Madison argued that smaller states often disregarded individual rights because one group could easily take power. A delegate from a large state threatened to pull out of the convention if the smaller states would not join under the Virginia Plan. Some of the smaller-state delegates had already threatened to leave.

Luther Martin of Maryland was a powerful spokesman for the small states. He refused to vote for the Virginia Plan because it implied that the small states were worth less than the large states: "The States have a right to an equality of representation. This is secured to us by our present articles of confederation; we are in possession of this privilege."[3]

Washington had been reluctant to lend his presence because he feared the convention would accomplish nothing. By now, he felt his reluctance had been justified. He called Martin and others from small states who opposed a large federal government narrow-minded.

however, the plan was rejected. Many believed it was too close to the Articles of Confederation.

On June 18, Alexander Hamilton proposed the British Plan. He hoped to model it after the British parliament. Hamilton was a wealthy, powerful politician. He was not convinced that the people could be trusted with the vote.

A New King?

Many delegates were concerned about who would rule the United States. They did not want another king. There was apparently a rumor that a plot had been hatched to invite Frederick, Duke of York, to become king of the United States. Frederick was King George III's second-oldest son.

Hamilton argued that with no property, ordinary citizens would not vote responsibly. If they had nothing to lose, they might be easily swayed to support policies that would adversely affect those who held property. Therefore, Hamilton wanted to trust only property-owning men with the vote. Hamilton pointed to the British government as the best in the world. Some members of the convention agreed that some sort of king would probably take power, even if they were personally opposed to the idea.

However, most delegates did not think it likely that a king would take power. Hamilton's plan was not seriously considered. It was too close to what the colonists had experienced under British rule.

William Pierce on Alexander Hamilton

William Pierce was not entirely complimentary in his remarks about Hamilton. "He is able, convincing, and engaging in his eloquence. . . . Yet there is something too feeble in his voice. . . . His manners [have] a degree of vanity that is highly disagreeable."[5]

Some state constitutions had even prohibited titles of nobility, saying they were too much like what their ancestors had left behind in England.

By June 28, not much progress had been made. Franklin made a motion that a preacher pray every morning before the convention "imploring the Assistance of Heaven."[4] Hugh Williamson of North Carolina, a wealthy physician, noted they had no money to pay a preacher. The motion was defeated. Many began to feel discouraged.

A portrait of politician Alexander Hamilton at his desk

Benjamin Franklin, Alexander Hamilton, and others meet in Philadelphia.

DEADLOCKS

On June 29, 1787, Oliver Ellsworth got to his feet. He planned to present an idea that might please the large states as well as the small states. His proposal later came to be called the Great Compromise.

Ellsworth's plan was to combine parts of both the Virginia and New Jersey plans. The idea was to create a bicameral legislature consisting of two separate lawmaking groups. One group would be the House of Representatives, or lower house. It would have members according to each state's population and would therefore tend to favor the larger states. For example, if Virginia had the largest population, it would have the largest number of representatives. The other group, called the Senate, or upper house, would have an equal number of representatives from each state, regardless of its population. For example, the large state Virginia and the small state Delaware would each receive the same number of votes. A bill would have to pass in both houses before being sent to the president, who would sign it into law or veto it. The delegates listened to Ellsworth lay out his plan, but a vote was postponed until later in the convention.

By the end of the day on July 2, the delegates were ready for a break. They did not meet on July 3 or 4. On Independence Day, which celebrated the signing of the Declaration of Independence 11 years earlier, the delegates attended a speech at nearby Race Street Church. On July 5, the delegates were back at work.

In 1789, when the House of Representatives held its first session, there were 65 representatives for all the states combined. After the census was taken for 1790, the number of representatives rose to 105 because of the increase in population. In 1911, the number was 435, the same number as today. The Constitution states that there cannot be more than one representative for every 30,000 people.

The Issue of Slavery

The Great Compromise, accepted on July 16, settled some of the problems between the small and large states. However, it revealed a fundamental split between the Northern and Southern states. The cause of this divide was slavery. This issue seemed at least as problematic as the number of representatives in the lower house. Yet it began with the seemingly unrelated issue of how to count the citizens of each state in order to allot the correct number of representatives. In 1787, however, the issue was cloudy because of enslaved African Americans.

According to the 1790 census, there were more than 40,000 slaves in the North and more than 650,000 slaves in the South. They were legally considered the property of the slaveholders. The conflict centered on whether, for the purposes of representation, slaves should be included in the population or not. The slaveholders wanted to count these slaves for purposes of getting more congressional representatives. Representatives from the Northern states wanted to count only free citizens of each state. They said slaves could not be counted as both property and people. The Northern states did not want to count slaves for representation, because that extra population would give the Southern states more power. The debates heated up again. It became clear that the Southern states would not agree to any constitution if slavery were outlawed.

A third proposal offered a compromise between the two sides, and it was accepted by the delegates. They agreed that the House of Representatives be based on the number of free persons—including women—and three-fifths of "all other persons." The phrase "all other persons" meant slaves.

So, though they had no rights, slaves were counted toward a state's population. Though women could not vote, they also were counted. The founders had definite ideas about who should hold power in

Outraged New Englanders

The issue of slavery would come up many times during the drafting of the Constitution. Many New Englanders felt strongly against the practice. Samuel Hopkins, a minister from Connecticut, was outraged when he heard about the compromise. He said, "How does it appear . . . that these States, who have been fighting for liberty and consider themselves as the highest and most noble example of zeal for it, cannot agree in any political constitution, unless it indulge and authorize them to inslave their fellow men."[1]

the new nation. They agreed that only landowners, usually white men, should be able to vote or hold office. Many of the delegates agreed with Hamilton that people would vote irresponsibly if they had no property.

Another part of the three-fifths compromise was that the slave trade could not be regulated by Congress for 20 years. Meanwhile, the existing Congress was considering legislation regarding slavery in new states. Britain had given the Northwest Territory to the United States after the Revolutionary War. This territory lay north of the Ohio River and west of the Appalachian Mountains. Several states were eventually created from it—Ohio, Indiana, Illinois, Michigan, Wisconsin, and part of Minnesota. Congress passed the Northwest Ordinance on July 13, 1787, which declared that slavery would not be allowed in these new states. However, that decision came at a price. In exchange for allowing a ban on slavery in the Northwest Territory, the Southern states were assured that slavery would continue to be legal in states that were created in the South.

On July 27, the Committee of Detail met. The committee chair was John Rutledge of

South Carolina. The other members were Oliver Ellsworth of Connecticut, Nathaniel Gorham of Massachusetts, Edmund Randolph of Virginia, and James Wilson of Pennsylvania. Their task was to take the 19 resolutions the convention had adopted and combine them in one document. The other delegates took a ten-day break. On August 6, the committee presented its first draft of the Constitution to the convention. The delegates began to look it over.

Although it had seemed to be solved, the topic of slavery came up

Avoiding the Issue

Glossing over the issue of slavery at the convention built up pressure within the United States over the following years. At the convention, the issue became so heated that it seemed a compromise would never be reached.

Although slavery remained legal after the convention, the issue did not go away. The pressure exploded with the American Civil War. Southern states seceded from the United States to start their own country. One of the main reasons these states seceded was over the issue of slavery and whether new states should be allowed to hold slaves.

These Southern states, called the Confederacy, fired on federal troops stationed at Fort Sumter in South Carolina. This marked the beginning of the Civil War on April 12, 1861. The war continued until 1865, when Confederate General Robert E. Lee surrendered to Union General Ulysses S. Grant at the Appomattox Court House in Virginia. More American men died in the Civil War than in any other war in U.S. history.

As a result of the war, slavery was abolished in the United States by the Thirteenth Amendment to the Constitution. Proposed January 31, 1865, the amendment was ratified on December 6, 1865.

again. On August 21, Luther Martin of Maryland
proposed a tax on imported slaves. This led to a
heated debate about whether slavery was moral.
The question had come up many times before. The
Declaration of Independence declared that "all men
are created equal."[2] Edmund Rutledge of South
Carolina said morality had nothing to do with the
issue. Roger Sherman wanted to drop the slavery
issue altogether, fearing it might cause the end of
the convention. Some slaveholders were against
unlimited importation of slaves from Africa and
the West Indies. But they worried that a federal
government might try to take away slave property
already held.

Some of the delegates strongly opposed slavery.
Benjamin Franklin, for example, was the president
of a prominent Philadelphia abolitionist society.
Although he had owned slaves while a young man, he
had come to regard slavery as evil.

Even some slaveholders, including George
Washington, did not like slavery. Curiously, despite
his words against slavery, Washington still kept slaves
instead of freeing them. In 1786, he said that it was
"among my first wishes to see some plan adopted
by the legislature, by which slavery in the Country

may be abolished by slow, sure and imperceptible degrees."[3]

The Southern states were equally adamant that the institution of slavery remain untouched. Once more, it looked as if a compromise might never be reached. If Franklin and other antislavery delegates had insisted on banning slavery, the Southern states might have left the convention, and the Constitution would never have been signed.

To keep the Southern states from leaving, a few decisions were reached. First, taxes would not be placed on goods exported to other countries. This concession primarily was made to benefit Northerners. In return, they agreed not to push for abolition. Second, slaves could be brought into the United States from other places for 20 years. After 1808, Congress would have the authority to ban the slave trade. The hope was that without new slaves from outside the states,

Washington and Runaway Slaves

Two of George Washington's slaves, Ona and Hercules, ran away from him. Washington's wife, Martha, wanted to pursue the slaves, but Washington disagreed. This incident was indicative of his attitude about slavery.

Lafayette and Slavery

The Marquis de Lafayette was a hero of the Revolutionary War. He was a Frenchman who came to the United States and fought alongside George Washington. He said, "I would never have drawn my sword in the cause of America if I could have conceived thereby that I was founding a land of slavery."[4]

slavery might die on its own. Third, Northern states would be bound by law to return any slaves that escaped from the South.

The delegates believed that remaining united was more important at the moment than outlawing slavery. The slavery question was resolved for the time. But it would not be long before it came up again.

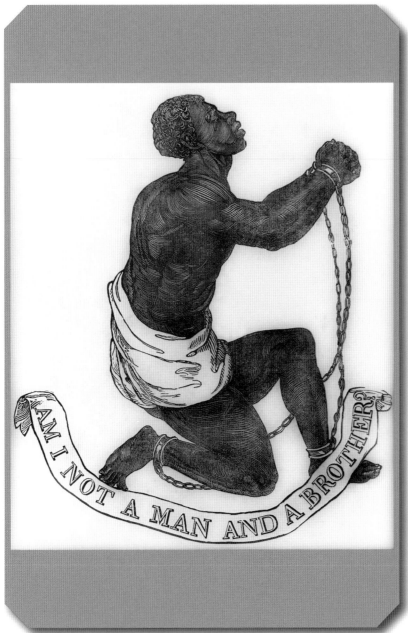

Slavery was a vital part of the Southern economy and a hotly debated issue during the framing of the Constitution.

King George III ruled England during the Revolutionary War. Many delegates worried about one person claiming too much power.

THE CONVENTION ENDS

Much had been accomplished. However, there was still one crucial decision to be made. What role and powers would the president have in the new government? Some delegates feared a president might gather too much power

and rule similarly to a king. They were thinking
about the king of Britain and the way he had
treated his American colonies. For this reason,
some wondered if there should be more than one
president. This could keep any one person from
becoming too powerful. Other delegates argued
that having more than one president would lead to
conflict among the leaders. They would naturally
try to gain as much power as possible, and nothing
would be accomplished. The delegates decided on
one president. They believed it would be clear to the
people that he was not a king.

The next issue was determining how to select the
president. One group wanted Congress to choose
the president. The president then would serve
seven years with no possibility of reelection. Other
suggestions included holding direct elections by the
people or allowing the state legislatures or governors
to choose the president. Each suggestion was strongly
opposed, and lengthy discussions about each
suggestion delayed the convention's progress.

Another Compromise

James Wilson of Pennsylvania proposed a
compromise: the states would choose a group of

Electoral College

Every state and the District of Columbia has a certain number of presidential electors. The number of electors equals the number of representatives from that state in the House of Representatives plus its two senators. However, the District of Columbia does not have full voting rights in the House or the Senate.

When people select a candidate by voting, they are also voting for the electors in their states. These electors then cast the actual votes on behalf of their states. Electors are bound to follow the will of the people. All the states require their electors to vote for the candidate with the most popular votes. Whichever presidential candidate receives the majority of electoral votes wins the election.

presidential electors. They would be chosen by their parties before the election. They would meet to choose the president. The electors would presumably know more about the candidates than the voters and cast better-informed votes. Whichever candidate received the most electoral votes would become president. Whoever received the second-most votes would become vice president. The president and vice president would serve terms of four years each. The delegates voted sixty times before Wilson's compromise was adopted.

The larger states were pleased because states with more citizens had more electors. The smaller states were pleased because the state legislatures would choose the electors. The House of Representatives would choose the president if the Electoral College gave no majority to a candidate. It was a good compromise.

By September 11, the Constitution was turned over to the Committee of Style and Arrangement. The committee would clean up the document and make sure everything was included that had been agreed upon.

On September 12, the delegates began to vote on each article of the Constitution. Some votes were close. But by now, many of the delegates had been working on the document for four months. The tired men could see an end, and this spurred their work. They were more willing to compromise.

Also on September 12, the inclusion of a bill of rights was proposed. Many states wanted this included, even though the Federalists, those who favored a strong federal government, did not think it necessary. This group included Madison, Washington, and Hamilton.

The motion was defeated. On September 15, concerned about the lack of a bill of rights, Edmund Randolph, George Mason, and Elbridge Gerry refused to support the Constitution. They proposed sending the Constitution back to the states

Jefferson's Thoughts on the Electoral College

Thomas Jefferson was not in favor of the Electoral College. He said, "I have ever considered the constitutional mode of election ultimately by the Legislature voting by States as the most dangerous blot in our Constitution, and one which some unlucky chance will some day hit and give us a pope and anti-pope."[1]

for consideration. This would have meant the states had to gather together again for another national Constitutional Convention. The motion was defeated.

The final draft of the Constitution was put to a vote. Ironically, Randolph had sat through the entire convention before refusing to sign. In addition to his feelings over the missing bill of rights, he was disappointed by how far the Constitution had veered from his original Virginia Plan. But Randolph's vote was

---

Amendments

Many of the delegates knew that the Constitution was not perfect. They included an article that allowed for the amendment of the Constitution. As of 2009, there were 27 amendments.

Some of these amendments are reflections on the way people's opinions have changed.

- The Fourteenth Amendment protects individual rights, defines citizenship, and punishes states for denying qualified citizens the right to vote. It was proposed on June 13, 1866, and ratified on July 9, 1868.
- The Fifteenth Amendment gave African-American men the right to vote. It was proposed February 26, 1869, and ratified on February 3, 1870.
- The Eighteenth Amendment prohibited the manufacturing and use of alcohol in the United States. This was also called Prohibition. It was proposed December 18, 1917, and ratified on January 16, 1919.
- The Nineteenth Amendment gave women the right to vote. It was proposed June 4, 1919, and was ratified on August 18, 1920.
- The Twenty-first Amendment repealed Prohibition. It was proposed by Congress February 20, 1933, and ratified on December 5, 1933.

not necessary. Thirty-nine of the fifty-five delegates signed the document. The Constitution passed.

George Washington sat in his wooden chair every time the convention delegates met. There was a small sun carved into the back of the chair. It was just visible above Washington's head. According to James Madison's notes, Franklin commented on the chair. He said,

> I have . . . often and often, in the course of the session . . . looked at that [sun] behind the President, without being able to tell whether it was rising or setting; but now at length, I have the happiness to know, that it is a rising, and not a setting sun.[2]

Washington was pleased that the Constitution had been approved. He saw a bright future for the states. The chair can still be seen today in the Philadelphia State House, or Independence Hall, as it is has come to be called.

William Pierce on Benjamin Franklin

William Pierce admired Franklin but with reservations. He wrote, "It is certain that he does not shine much in public Council. He is no speaker, nor does he seem to let politics engage his attention. He is, however, a most extraordinary Man, and tells a story in a style more engaging than anything I ever heard. . . . He is 82 years old, and possesses an activity of mind equal to a youth of 25 years."[3]

RATIFICATION

On September 17, 1787, the weary delegates met for the last session of the convention. They had worked intensely to blend the views of so many people into one document.

The delegates formally ended the convention at 4:00 p.m. that day. They walked to a nearby restaurant named City Tavern for a final meal as a group.

The next step, before the Constitution could go into effect, was to have the document ratified by at least nine states. As the delegates left for home, they must have wondered about the chances for the document to be ratified. On one hand, the states had powerful arguments against the Constitution. People did not completely trust a powerful central government that seemed far away from their everyday lives. Additionally, most Americans disliked the thought of being taxed by that government, as the British had taxed them. Finally, local politicians would fight the Constitution aggressively to keep their own power. On the other hand, George Washington was a powerful supporter of ratification. Along with that, most people already believed the Articles of Confederation were too weak, and

A reconstruction of City Tavern, where the delegates ate meals during the Constitutional Convention

therefore, another document was needed. The situation looked uncertain but hopeful.

Two local printers, David Claypoole and John Dunlap, were responsible for printing the Constitution. They had to work fast and all through the night because they needed many copies quickly. By morning, they intended to have copies ready.

These would be sent out to the states. State conventions would then use the copies as a starting point for debate. The states would either ratify the Constitution or reject it.

Madison wrote a letter to Jefferson about how hard it had been for the delegates to agree on the document. He said that bringing the opposing viewpoints together had been "a task more difficult than can be well conceived by those who were not concerned in the execution of it." Not all the delegates were certain that the Constitution was the best form of government. However, as Madison believed, it was the best available under the circumstances. Madison later wrote, "That which is the least imperfect is therefore the best government."[4]

On September 28, Congress approved the Constitution. The Constitution then was sent to the individual state conventions. These groups would vote on whether they would ratify the document. Approximately 1,200 state delegates had been chosen by their states. They held the fate of the Constitution in their hands.

The U.S. Constitution

John Adams was a Federalist.

RATIFICATION

Before the Constitution would be ratified
by the states, there was much discussion
and debate about whether it should be approved.

On October 5, under the name Centinel,
Samuel Bryan published the first Anti-Federalist

Paper in Philadelphia's *Independent Gazetteer*. Bryan felt strongly about the lack of a bill of rights and the way the Constitution took over states' rights. He feared that a small group of wealthy leaders would control the new government. He worried they would ignore the needs of the common people.

The Revolutionary War had been fought against precisely this sort of remote government. Bryan particularly was concerned about Congress having both the power to raise taxes and to require a large permanent army. He argued that this gave Congress the power to raise taxes as high as it wanted, which would become a burden to the very citizens it was supposed to protect. It would then use the army to collect those taxes, by force if necessary.

In reply to Bryan's paper, James Wilson delivered a speech the next day praising the new government as the best the world had ever seen. Wilson had attended the Constitutional Convention and was a strong supporter of the new document. He said, "I am satisfied that anything nearer to perfection could not have been accomplished."[1] Point by point, he argued against Bryan's fears.

Wilson was not the only one to argue against the Anti-Federalists. On October 27, the first of 85

Federalist Papers was published in New York City under the pseudonym Publius. Alexander Hamilton collaborated with John Jay and James Madison to write them. The papers showed why the Articles of Confederation did not work. They helped people understand that the Constitution could be amended.

Widely respected and well-known, both George Washington and Benjamin Franklin favored the new Constitution. Their support carried nearly as much weight as the arguments of the Federalists.

But the opposition continued. The Anti-Federalists argued mostly from the point of view of states' rights. Their main arguments were centered on the lack of a bill of rights and some laws about trade and business that worked against the South. They also feared the new government would set the rich against the poor.

One Anti-Federalist argued that the territory of the 13 states was too large to govern. He felt the government would be unresponsive and unrepresentative. Madison argued against this by saying the larger the republic, the less chance any one group could dominate the government.

By late May 1788, the 85 Federalist Papers were collected and published under the title *The Federalist*. These essays persuaded U.S. citizens that the Constitution was a good solution.

RATIFICATION BEGINS

The first state to vote on ratifying the Constitution was Delaware. On December 7, 1787, the delegates from that state unanimously ratified the document.

On December 12, 1787, Pennsylvania ratified the Constitution by 46 to 23. However, Anti-Federalists continued to voice their concerns. Anti-Federalists broke up a Federalist celebration, burned a copy of the Constitution, and physically attacked some Federalists.

Three more states quickly voted to ratify the Constitution. New Jersey unanimously ratified the Constitution on December 18, 1787. Georgia also unanimously ratified

The Supporters

In general, the Federalists were made up of farmers with large amounts of property, business leaders, and wealthy educated people. The Anti-Federalists were usually small farmers and men who owned and operated small businesses.

THE

FEDERALIST:

ADDRESSED TO THE

PEOPLE OF THE STATE OF
NEW-YORK.

NUMBER I.

Introduction.

The Federalist *supported the ratification of the Constitution.*

it on January 2, 1788. On January 9, Connecticut ratified it by a wide margin.

The Massachusetts convention ratified the Constitution on February 6, 1788. But the process had not been smooth. John Hancock, who had signed the Declaration of Independence, was president of the Massachusetts convention. He felt pressure from both Federalists and Anti-Federalists. He could not decide how he should vote. When some Federalists told him he might be offered the vice presidency or even the presidency, he voted for the

Constitution. In the end, Massachusetts ratified 187 to 168, but the state leaders added an amendment that called for a bill of rights to be included in the Constitution.

Six of the seven remaining states added similar recommendations to their ratifications. The lack of a national bill of rights had concerned the Anti-Federalists from the beginning of the convention. When states recommended adding such a bill, it was a victory for the Anti-Federalists.

The next two states to vote had major objections to the Constitution. On March 24, 1788, Rhode Island took its first of two votes. It rejected the Constitution in a statewide vote. Of the state's eligible voters, 237 voted in favor and 2,708 voted against. In New Hampshire, Federalists adjourned the ratifying convention when it looked as if the Constitution would not be ratified. The setbacks in these two states caused Federalists to fear that the Constitution might not be adopted after all.

However, on April 28, 1788, the Federalists again could celebrate. Maryland ratified the Constitution by a large margin: 63 to 11. A few weeks later, South Carolina became the eighth state to ratify the Constitution. According to the rules laid out by the convention, only one additional state needed to ratify the Constitution. It then would become law.

Then, on June 21, 1788, New Hampshire met again. It became the ninth state to ratify, which it did by only ten votes. With the approval of nine states, the Constitution was officially ratified.

Although the Constitution could now go into effect, it was not clear whether the United States could still work as a nation because neither New York nor Virginia had ratified it yet. Without these two states, many people believed the

Political Parties

The Federalists were one of the first formal political groups in the United States. Alexander Hamilton was one of the Federalist Party's foremost leaders. George Washington, the first president of the United States, was not a member of a political party, but his views were sympathetic toward the Federalists.

The second president of the United States, John Adams, was a Federalist. The Federalists had control of the U.S. government from 1789 to 1801, but the party disappeared in the 1820s.

Thomas Jefferson, who served as Adams's vice president and later as the third president of the United States, had many views that aligned with the Anti-Federalists. When he became president in 1801, the Anti-Federalists gained power. Jefferson reversed a few of the Federalist policies that had previously taxed farmers. The Anti-Federalists later became known as Democrat-Republicans. Many of these Democrat-Republicans were farmers, plantation owners, or tradesmen. When the Federalist Party broke up in the 1820s, the Democrat-Republicans also split into various groups. Some believe that one of these groups became what is today the Democratic Party. Today's Republican Party has roots that trace back to the 1850s.

United States could not succeed. On June 25, 1788, Virginia voted to ratify the Constitution. Passage in Virginia overcame a major hurdle. The large, influential state linked the North and South.

On July 26, 1788, with a margin of only three votes, New York ratified the Constitution. Its approval had been critical. At the same time, New York's approval was qualified. Like other states, it stipulated that a bill of rights must be added. On September 11, 1788, the Congress voted to accept the Constitution and put it into effect.

THE OPERATIONAL CONSTITUTION

March 4, 1789, was the day when the Constitution began to be followed as the supreme U.S. law. On April 30, Congress met again. Only this time, it was not the Continental Congress, trying desperately to keep the states together under the articles, without enough money or authority. This time the new Congress met under the authority of the new Constitution.

Even though not all the states had yet ratified the Constitution, George Washington was serving as the first president of the United States. The election had taken place on February 4, 1789, and Washington was inaugurated on April 30. John Adams, who had signed the Declaration of Independence for Massachusetts, received the second most electoral votes. He became Washington's vice president.

Among the many others chosen for office was Alexander Hamilton. He was to be Washington's secretary of the treasury. He wanted to have the government take over the war debts of the Northern states, and then to start a national bank. These ideas worried Southern lawmakers. They thought he was helping the government take on too much power.

George Washington Helps Sway the Vote

Along with the Virginia Federalists, George Washington had added his support to ratification in his home state.

On June 25, 1788, Virginia voted to ratify the Constitution. It was a close vote—89 in favor of the Constitution and 79 against. Virginia also added some amendments to be considered. Thomas Jefferson later wrote he believed it would not have passed without Washington's support.

Hamilton agreed to a compromise with Southern states. If they would support his financial ideas, he would use his influence to locate a new national capital city in a Southern state. He kept his promise and helped locate Washington DC in the South. Both Virginia and Maryland gave up some territory to create the District of Columbia along the Potomac River. The government officially moved there in 1800.

A 1788 New York celebration honors Alexander Hamilton and the adoption of the Constitution.

George Washington was inaugurated as the first president of the United States on April 30, 1789.

THE BILL OF RIGHTS

ongress adopted the Bill of Rights in September 1789. This was the event the last two states had been waiting for. North Carolina ratified the Constitution on November 21, 1789. On May 29, 1790, Rhode Island held its second ratifying convention. It ratified the Constitution in a vote of 34–32, the smallest margin of ratification of any state. It was the thirteenth and final state to ratify the document.

Creating the Bill of Rights had been a lengthy process. The new U.S. Congress began by responding to more than 80 proposals for amendments that the state ratifying conventions had suggested. James Madison, elected to the House of Representatives, took on the task of paring down the list.

In June 1789, Madison sent 17 amendments to Congress, which then trimmed these to 12. Copies of the 12 amendments were sent to the states for approval. According to Article V of the Constitution, three-fourths of the states needed to ratify an amendment for it to be accepted. Ten of the twelve amendments sent to the states were accepted. On December 15, 1791, these ten amendments were incorporated into the Constitution. They are known as the Bill of Rights.

THE BILL OF RIGHTS

The Bill of Rights outlines what the Founding Fathers believed to be the fundamental rights of people in the United States. The amendments also ensure that the federal government does not overstep the boundaries that are outlined for it in the Constitution. These freedoms, however, do not come without limits. The U.S. Supreme Court interprets these provisions and applies them to cases that arise in the legal system.

There has been some difficulty in interpreting the Constitution. Some people believe in a strict interpretation of these amendments, in which the people enjoy only those liberties specified in the amendments. Some, however, believe that the Constitution should be interpreted more broadly. They believe individuals have more liberties than are provided for explicitly in the Constitution. They believe the Bill of Rights protects some freedoms that are not specifically mentioned.

With great privilege comes great responsibility. While the Bill of Rights grants the people of the United States many freedoms, these freedoms are not without limit. Citizens cannot use their freedoms to hurt others. For example, a person cannot yell out "fire" in a theater full of people when there is no fire. Also, students cannot bring guns to school.

First Amendment advocates rally to protest the jailing of a New York Times journalist who refused to reveal her sources to a jury.

FIRST AMENDMENT

Congress shall make no law respecting an establishment of religion, or prohibiting the free exercise thereof; or abridging the freedom of speech, or of the press; or the right of the people peaceably to assemble, and to petition the Government for a redress of grievances.

To many U.S. citizens, the First Amendment is the most familiar. It provides for the freedom of religion, speech, press, the right to assemble, and the freedom to petition the government. Many of these freedoms are exclusive to countries in which the land is governed by the people.

But this amendment is also one of the most debated. For example, a person generally cannot spread false information about another person that is damaging to that person's reputation. This is called libel. Language that provokes violence can also be restricted.

Second Amendment

A well regulated Militia, being necessary to the security of a free State, the right of the people to keep and bear Arms, shall not be infringed.

The Second Amendment is often known as "the right to bear arms." This amendment provides for the right of each state to have a militia, which is composed of citizens who also serve as soldiers. Many people believe this amendment also gives each private citizen the right to own a gun, but others disagree and believe the amendment only applies to the military.

Third Amendment

No Soldier shall, in time of peace be quartered in any house, without the consent of the Owner, nor in time of war, but in a manner to be prescribed by law.

In the 1700s, British soldiers often stayed in the homes of private citizens. Citizens did not like housing these soldiers. The Third Amendment restricts this practice during peacetime. It does, however, allow the practice in times of war when national security might take precedence over personal freedom.

Fourth Amendment

The right of the people to be secure in their persons, houses, papers, and effects, against unreasonable searches and seizures, shall not be violated, and no Warrants shall issue, but upon probable cause, supported by Oath or affirmation, and particularly describing the place to be searched, and the persons or things to be seized.

The Fourth Amendment restricts the government from entering private homes and arresting citizens without a warrant. Justice Louis Brandeis said the Fourth Amendment protected "the right to be left alone."[1]

Exclusionary Rule

The exclusionary rule is a legal principle that relates to Fourth Amendment rights. According to the exclusionary rule, evidence that is obtained by an illegal search cannot be used in a trial. This is a controversial issue, because this evidence is sometimes necessary in order to convict a criminal. There are some exceptions to the rule. The concept was established to encourage law enforcement officials to conduct proper searches and obtain warrants.

Since 1789, more than 10,000 amendments to the Constitution have been proposed. However, only a fraction of those proposals have had enough support to go through the ratification process. And of those few, an even smaller number have been added to the Constitution. Some of the amendments that did not pass include:

• Rename the United States the "United States of the Earth" (1893).

• Make marriage between races illegal (1912).

• Make divorce illegal (1914).

• Limit one person's wealth to $1 million (1933).

• Put all acts of war to national vote. Those who vote yes would have to register for service in the army (1916).

The British government had used general warrants that allowed them to search broad areas, but the Fourth Amendment calls for a specific warrant in order to search a home or a citizen. In some instances, however, searches can occur without a warrant. For example, if illegal narcotics are visible in a car, police may search it.

Fifth Amendment

No person shall be held to answer for a capital, or otherwise infamous crime, unless on a presentment or indictment of a Grand Jury, except in cases arising in the land or naval forces, or in the Militia, when in actual service in time of War or public danger; nor shall any person be subject for the same offence to be twice put in jeopardy of life or limb; nor shall be compelled in any criminal case to be a witness against himself, nor be deprived of life, liberty, or property, without due process of law; nor shall private property be taken for public use, without just compensation.

The Fifth Amendment outlines the rights and processes for people accused of a crime. It limits the power of the government in trying these people. The Fifth Amendment also prevents a person from being tried twice for the same crime. This is called "double jeopardy."

This amendment includes language that protects a person from self-incrimination. This means a person has the right to remain silent, and the silence cannot be assumed to mean the person is guilty. This is why people "plead the fifth."

The Fifth Amendment gives "due process of law," which is the right to a fair trial. The Amendment also addresses issues of eminent domain—when private property is used for public purposes. The government is not allowed to take private property without providing "just compensation."

Sixth Amendment

In all criminal prosecutions, the accused shall enjoy the right to a speedy and public trial, by an impartial jury of the State and district wherein the crime shall have been committed, which district shall have been previously ascertained by law, and to be informed of the nature and cause of the accusation;

The Supreme Court

The Supreme Court was established in the Constitution. Originally, it had six members: five associate justices and one chief justice. It now has nine members: eight associate justices and one chief justice.

Supreme Court justices have no limits on how long they can serve. If a justice retires or dies while in office, the U.S. president nominates a new justice, who goes through confirmation hearings by the U.S. Senate.

to be confronted with the witnesses against him; to have compulsory process for obtaining witnesses in his favor, and to have the Assistance of Counsel for his defence.

The Sixth Amendment also applies to people accused of a crime. During a trial, the accused has the right to an "impartial jury" that is made up of people who are not connected to the crime. This amendment also declares that the trial must be speedy and public. This helps keep the integrity of the trial—it cannot be done in secret, and evidence and witnesses must be presented in a timely manner. The defendant also has the right to an attorney.

Seventh Amendment

In Suits at common law, where the value in controversy shall exceed twenty dollars, the right of trial by jury shall be preserved, and no fact tried by a jury, shall be otherwise re-examined in any Court of the United States, than according to the rules of the common law.

The Seventh Amendment provides for the proceedings in civil cases, or noncriminal cases in which private parties dispute matters such as a contract, employment discrimination, or an injury. The Seventh Amendment also outlines the roles of the jury and the judge. In short, in most cases the judge presides over the trial and the jury decides the verdict.

Eighth Amendment

Excessive bail shall not be required, nor excessive fines imposed, nor cruel and unusual punishments inflicted.

The wording for the Eighth Amendment reads very closely to the 1689 English Bill of Rights. The Eighth Amendment gives prisoners the right to a reasonable bail amount. Bail is the money paid so the defendant can leave jail during the time prior to his or her trial. The Eighth Amendment is where the phrase "cruel and unusual punishment" comes from. It was intended to make particularly violent forms of punishment illegal, such as torture. Today, many courts use this phrase to ensure that a punishment fits a crime.

Ninth Amendment

The enumeration in the Constitution, of certain rights, shall not be construed to deny or disparage others retained by the people.

This amendment states that people in the United States have more rights than those that are specifically outlined in the Bill of Rights. The writers did not want the Bill of Rights to be interpreted as a comprehensive list.

Tenth Amendment

The powers not delegated to the United States by the Constitution, nor prohibited by it to the States, are reserved to the States respectively, or to the people.[2]

When the Constitutional Convention was meeting in Philadelphia, debates raged over the balance of power between the federal government and the states. The Tenth Amendment clarifies that the federal government's power is limited to what is outlined in the Constitution. The states can claim powers not outlined in the Constitution. This amendment has been debated throughout the years as the courts interpret the Constitution strictly or broadly.

THE CONSTITUTION TODAY

The Constitution has survived because of its flexibility. Incredibly, it is only 4,543 words long, including signatures. It is specific enough to allow our country to have used it for more than 200 years. But it is also general enough for people to be able to interpret it in ways that make it applicable for changing times.

The entire four-page Constitution is displayed in the Rotunda at the National Archives Building. The document is in a special encasement. In the past, only the first and last pages had been displayed. Today,

The Constitution Travels

The day after the Constitution was signed, a copy was sent to Congress in New York City. For many years, the secretary of state took care of that original. In 1800, the Constitution was moved to the permanent capital, Washington DC. But during the War of 1812, British soldiers invaded Washington. The Constitution was in danger of being burned, so it was carried out of the city and into Virginia. In 1814, the document was returned to the capital after the war. It was wrapped and placed in a steel case until 1901.

That year, the Library of Congress became the home of the Constitution. There, its pages were kept in a safe. In 1941, the Constitution was moved to a specially constructed display case. But in late 1941, the Japanese attacked Pearl Harbor and the United States entered World War II. Fearing that the U.S. capital might be attacked, the Constitution was again moved. It was placed in Fort Knox, Kentucky, until 1944. Since then, it has been moved back to the Library of Congress and is displayed at the National Archives building.

the Constitution is part of an exhibit that also includes the Declaration of Independence and the Bill of Rights.

THE TEST OF TIME

The men of the Constitutional Convention created rules that fit the circumstances of their times. The ensuing amendments to the Constitution made major changes over the centuries. Slavery was abolished, women gained the right to vote, and alcohol was made illegal and then legal again. But the structure of the Constitution allowed for these changes to be made in a regulated manner.

The delegates managed to give enough power to a central government to effectively manage trade, the military, and other matters of national importance. At the same time, they managed to protect people's individual liberties. The Constitution has become the ideal for many people around the world. It has withstood the test of time. ⌐

*The entire U.S. Constitution is displayed in the Rotunda at the National
Archives building in Washington DC.*

TIMELINE

1783

The United States and Great Britain sign the Treaty of Paris to end the Revolutionary War on September 3.

August 1786– February 1787

Shays's Rebellion takes place.

1787

The Great Compromise is adopted on July 16.

1787

The delegations from all 12 states approve the Constitution on September 17. Thirty-nine delegates sign it, officially ending the convention.

1787

The first Federalist Paper essay is published on October 27 in New York's *Independent Journal*.

1786

The Annapolis Convention begins in September.

1787

The Constitutional Convention opens in Philadelphia on May 25.

1787

Congress passes the Northwest Ordinance to create a process for creating new states on July 13.

1787

Delaware becomes the first state to ratify the Constitution on December 7.

1788

New Hampshire becomes the ninth state to ratify the Constitution on June 21. The Constitution becomes effective.

1789

The first presidential election takes place on February 4.

TIMELINE

1789	1789	1789
On March 4, the first Congress under the Constitution meets in New York City, the temporary U.S. capital city.	George Washington is sworn in as the first president of the United States on April 30.	James Madison introduces the proposed Bill of Rights in the House of Representatives on June 8.

1789	1790
New Jersey is the first state to ratify the Bill of Rights on November 20.	On May 29, Rhode Island becomes the last state to ratify the Constitution.

1789

On September 11, Alexander Hamilton is appointed secretary of the treasury.

1789

On September 25, Congress approves 12 amendments and sends them to the states for ratification.

1790

The U.S. capital moves from New York to Philadelphia on December 6.

1791

Virginia ratifies the Bill of Rights on December 15. Ten of the twelve proposed amendments become part of the U.S. Constitution.

Essential Facts

Date of Event

1787–1789

Place of Event

Philadelphia, Pennsylvania

Key Players

- ❖ Benjamin Franklin
- ❖ Alexander Hamilton
- ❖ James Madison
- ❖ Edmund Randolph
- ❖ George Washington

Highlights of Event

❖ The Great Compromise was adopted on July 16, 1787. It was meant to please large and small states with how representatives are chosen for a new Congress.

❖ The delegations from all 12 states approved the Constitution on September 17, 1787. Thirty-nine delegates signed it, officially ending the convention. The delegates did not think it was perfect but believed it was the best document available under the circumstances.

❖ Delaware became the first state to ratify the Constitution on December 7, 1787. It did so by unanimous vote.

❖ The first presidential election took place on February 4, 1789. George Washington won the presidency. John Adams, who came in second place, became vice president. George Washington was sworn in as the first president of the United States on April 30, 1789.

❖ James Madison introduced the proposed Bill of Rights in the House of Representatives on June 8, 1789.

❖ Virginia ratified the Bill of Rights on December 15, 1791. Ten of the twelve proposed amendments became part of the U.S. Constitution.

Quote

"I am satisfied that anything nearer to perfection could not have been accomplished."—*James Wilson on the U.S. Constitution*

Additional Resources

Select Bibliography

Dunn, Susan, ed. *Something That Will Surprise the World: The Essential Writings of the Founding Fathers*. New York: Basic Books, 2006.

Ellis, Joseph J. *American Creation: Triumphs and Tragedies at the Founding of the Republic*. New York: Knopf, 2007.

Ellis, Joseph J. *Founding Brothers: The Revolutionary Generation*. New York: Vintage, 2000.

Kaminski, John P. *A Necessary Evil?: Slavery and the Debate over the Constitution*. Madison, WI: Madison House, 1995.

Further Reading

Fradin, Dennis Brindell. *The Founders: The 39 Stories Behind the U.S. Constitution*. New York: Walker, 2005.

Hubbard-Brown, Janet. *How the Constitution Was Created*. New York: Chelsea House, 2007.

Moehn, Heather. *The U.S. Constitution: A Primary Source Investigation into the Fundamental Law of the United States*. New York: Rosen, 2003.

Ritchie, Donald A., and JusticeLearning.org. *Our Constitution*. New York: Oxford University Press, 2006.

Web Links

To learn more about the U.S. Constitution and
Bill of Rights, visit ABDO Publishing Company online
at **www.abdopublishing.com**. Web sites about the U.S.
Constitution and Bill of Rights are featured on our Book
Links page. These links are routinely monitored and
updated to provide the most current information available.

Places to Visit

Independence National Historical Park
143 South Third Street, Philadelphia, PA 19106
800-537-7676
www.nps.gov/index
Visit the historical landmark where the Declaration of
Independence and the U.S. Constitution were signed.

The James Madison Museum
129 Caroline Street, Orange, VA 22960-1532
540-672-1776
www.jamesmadisonmus.org
This museum is dedicated to the "father of the Constitution." The
museum displays many of Madison's personal possessions.

National Archives and Records Administration (NARA)
700 Pennsylvania Avenue, Northwest, Washington, DC 20408
866-272-6272
www.archives.gov
The National Archives and Records Administration building
displays the U.S. Constitution and other important U.S.
documents.

GLOSSARY

amend
> To change.

Anti-Federalist
> Someone who did not support the U.S. Constitution, fearing it would create a too-powerful federal government.

Articles of Confederation
> An agreement among the states to work together. The Articles of Confederation governed prior to the U.S. Constitution.

bicameral legislature
> A form of government with two houses of lawmakers.

Congress of the Confederation
> The legislature that existed under the Articles of Confederation.

Continental Congress
> The governing body before and during the Revolutionary War.

convention
> A gathering of people with a similar interest or profession.

Federalist
> Someone who supported the U.S. Constitution and a strong federal government.

guerilla tactics
> Irregular fighting practices that include fighting from behind shelter and using ambushes.

legislature
> A lawmaking body.

militia
> A group of part-time soldiers who train to fight in emergencies.

Prohibition
>   A constitutional amendment that forbade the manufacture and
>   use of alcohol.

ratify
>   To approve.

repeal
>   To take back a law that has already been passed.

secede
>   To withdraw.

traitor
>   Someone who acts against his or her own country.

treaty
>   A legal agreement between two countries.

Treaty of Paris
>   The legal agreement that the United States and Great Britain
>   signed in 1783 to end the Revolutionary War.

unanimous
>   When everyone involved is in agreement.

veto
>   To deny a law passed by a lawmaking body.

Source Notes

Chapter 1. Those Arguing Patriots
1. "The Charters of Freedom: Declaration of Independence" *National Archives and Records Administration*. 9 Mar. 2009 <http://www. archives.gov/exhibits/charters/declaration_transcript.html>.
2. Hannah Winthrop Chapter NSDAR. *An Historic Guide to Cambridge*. Cambridge, MA: Hannah Winthrop Chapter NSDAR, 1907. 86–87.

Chapter 2. What Came Before
1. Alan Bearman. "Stamp Act." *World Book Online Reference Center*. 27 Feb. 2009 <http://worldbook.com/wb/Article?id=ar528680>.

Chapter 3. Chaos and Confusion
1. "A More Perfect Union: The Creation of the U.S. Constitution." *National Archives and Records Administration*. 9 Mar. 2009 <http://www.archives.gov/exhibits/charters/constitution_history. html>.
2. "The Papers of George Washington." George Washington to John Jay, 15 August 1786 (The Papers, Confederation Series, 4:212-13). *University of Virginia*. 13 Mar. 2009 <http://gwpapers. virginia.edu/documents/constitution/1784/index.html>.
3. William C. Rives. *History of the Life and Times of James Madison*. Boston: Little, Brown, 1866. 102.

Chapter 4. Convention Attendees
1. William Pierce. "Character Sketches of Delegates to the Federal Convention." *The Records of the Federal Convention of 1787 CXIX*. 10 Mar. 2009 <http://memory.loc.gov/cgi-bin/query/r?ammem/hlaw:@ field(DOCID+@lit(fr003134))>.
2. "Madison Debates." *Avalon Project*. 10 Mar. 2009 <http://avalon. law.yale.edu/18th_century/debates_917.asp>.

Chapter 5. The Convention Begins

1. Richard B. Bernstein. *Thomas Jefferson.* New York: Oxford
University Press, 2003. 71.
2. William Pierce. "Character Sketches of Delegates to the Federal
Convention." *The Records of the Federal Convention of 1787 CXIX.* 10 Mar.
2009 <http://memory.loc.gov/cgi-bin/query/r?ammem/hlaw:@
field(DOCID+@lit(fr003134))>.
3. "Luther Martin: Genuine Information III." *Teaching American
History.org.* 10 Mar. 2009 <http://www.teachingamericanhistory.
org/library/index.asp?document=2103>.
4. "Benjamin Franklin FAQ." *Franklin Institute.* 10 Mar. 2009
<http://sln.fi.edu/franklin/birthday/faq.html>.
5. William Pierce. "Character Sketches of Delegates to the Federal
Convention." *The Records of the Federal Convention of 1787 CXIX.* 10 Mar.
2009 <http://memory.loc.gov/cgi-bin/query/r?ammem/hlaw:@
field(DOCID+@lit(fr003134))>.

Chapter 6. Deadlocks

1. John P. Kaminski. *A Necessary Evil?: Slavery and the Debate over the
Constitution.* Madison, WI: Madison House, 1995. 95.
2. "The Declaration of Independence." *USHistory.org.* 9 Mar. 2009
<http://www.ushistory.org/Declaration/document/index.htm>.
3. Joseph J. Ellis. *Founding Brothers: The Revolutionary Generation.* New
York: Vintage Books, 2000.113.
4. Fritz Herschfield. *George Washington and Slavery: A Documentary Portrayal.*
Columbia, MO: University of Missouri Press. 121.

Source Notes Continued

Chapter 7. The Convention Ends
1. John P. Foley, ed. *The Jeffersonian Cyclopedia*. New York: Funk and Wagnalls, 1900. 715.
2. James Madison. *Columbia Encyclopedia,* sixth ed. 9 Mar. 2009 <http://www.bartleby.com/73/323.html>.
3. William Pierce. "Character Sketches of Delegates to the Federal Convention." *The Records of the Federal Convention of 1787 CXIX.* 10 Mar. 2009 <http://memory.loc.gov/cgi-bin/query/r?ammem/hlaw:@field(DOCID+@lit(fr003134))>.
4. "A More Perfect Union: The Creation of the U.S. Constitution." *National Archives and Records Administration.* 9 Mar. 2009 <http://www.archives.gov/exhibits/charters/constitution_history.html>.
5. David Colbert, ed. *Eyewitness to America.* New York: Pantheon Books 1997. 101.

Chapter 8. Ratification
1. "Speech of James Wilson, October 6, 1787." *USConstitution.org.* 10 Mar. 2009 <http://www.constitution.org/afp/jwilson0.htm>.
2. James Madison. "The Federalist Number 10." *Constitution.org.* 10 Mar. 2009 <http://www.constitution.org/fed/federa10.htm>.

Chapter 9. The Bill of Rights
1. Monk, Linda R. *The Words We Live By: Your Annotated Guide to the Constitution*. New York: Hyperion, 2003. 157.
2. "Bill of Rights." *Archives.gov.* 9 Mar. 2009 <http://www.archives.gov/exhibits/charters/bill_of_rights_transcript.html>.

INDEX

abolition, 58–59

Adams, John, 20, 39, 78, 80

Annapolis Convention, 31

Anti-Federalist Papers, 72–73

Anti-Federalists, 72–77, 78

Appomattox Court House, 57

Articles of Confederation, 18–21, 25, 27, 28, 30–31, 32, 42, 47, 48, 49, 68, 74, 79

Articles of War, 21

Bill of Rights, 82–94. *See also individual amendments*

Boston Massacre, 17, 20

Braddock, Edward, 17

Britain, 7–10, 14–17, 27, 30, 36, 56, 63

British parliament, 9, 16, 49

British Plan, 49

broad interpretation, 84, 92

Bryan, Samuel, 72–73

census, 54

Centinel, 72

checks and balances, 36

Chesapeake Bay, 9

City Tavern, 68

Civil War, 57

Claypoole, David, 69

colonies, 7–8, 10, 16–19, 20, 22, 26, 63

Committee of Detail, 56

Committee of Style and Arrangement, 65

Committees of Correspondence, 17

Confederacy, 57

Continental army, 7, 9, 20, 21–22, 25

Cornwallis, Charles, 9, 22

currency, 26–27

Dayton, Jonathan, 40

debts, 16, 22, 26, 28, 80

Declaration of Independence, 8, 10, 12, 39, 53, 58, 76, 80, 94

Dickinson, John, 40

Dunlap, John, 69

Eighteenth Amendment, 66

Eighth Amendment, 91

Electoral College, 64, 65

Ellsworth, Oliver, 52–53, 56

exchange rates, 26, 27

federal government, 19, 26, 35, 48, 58, 65, 84, 92

Federalist, The, 74, 75

Federalist Papers, 74, 75

Federalists, 65, 74–77, 78, 80

Fifteenth Amendment, 66

Fifth Amendment, 88–89

First Amendment, 85–86

First Continental Congress, 7, 39

Fourteenth Amendment, 66

Fourth Amendment, 87–88

France, 14–15, 16, 24, 27, 39

Index Continued

Franklin, Benjamin, 7, 11, 37, 39, 40, 44, 50, 58, 59, 67, 70, 74
French and Indian War, 15, 16, 17, 19, 22

George III (king of England), 8, 49
Gorham, Nathaniel, 56
Grant, Ulysses S., 57
Great Compromise, 52–54
guerilla warfare, 16–17, 21

Hamilton, Alexander, 31, 32, 39, 49, 50, 56, 65, 74, 78, 80
Hancock, John, 76
Henry, Patrick, 36
House of Representatives, 53, 54, 55, 64, 83

immigrants, 36
Independence Hall. *See* Philadelphia State House
inflation, 26

Jackson, William, 43
Jay, John, 74
Jefferson, Thomas, 39, 40, 45, 65, 70, 78, 80

kings, 8, 9, 10, 14, 16, 28, 31, 36, 49, 63

Lafayette, Marquis de, 60
Lee, Robert E., 57

Madison, James, 31, 32, 34–35, 36, 38, 39, 65, 70
  Bill of Rights, 83
  Federalist Papers, 74
  notes at convention, 43, 67
  Virginia Plan, 46, 48
Martin, Luther, 48, 57
Mason, George, 39–40, 65
Mifflin, Thomas, 12
militias, 8–9, 11, 25, 26, 29, 30, 86, 88
Morris, Gouverneur, 40
Morris, Robert, 7, 43

National Archives Building, 93
New Jersey Plan, 48–49, 53
Nineteenth Amendment, 66
Ninth Amendment, 92
nobility, 50
Northwest Territory, 56

Paterson, William, 48
Penn, William, 7
Philadelphia, Pennsylvania, 6, 7, 11, 12, 31, 35, 39, 43, 58, 73, 92
Philadelphia State House, 12, 42, 44, 67
Pierce, William, 35, 46, 50, 67
prayer, 50
president of the United States, 10, 36, 46, 53, 62–64, 90. *See also specific presidents*
Publius, 74

Quakers, 7, 37

Randolph, Edmund, 45–46,
   57, 65, 66
ratification of the Constitution,
   68–70, 72–80, 82–83
Redcoats, 16–17, 22
Revolutionary War, 7–9, 12,
   16–17, 20, 21, 24, 26, 28,
   31, 39, 56, 60, 73
Rutledge, Edmund, 58
Rutledge, John, 56

Second Amendment, 86
Second Continental Congress,
   8, 39
secrecy, 44–45, 90
Senate, 36, 53, 90
Seventh Amendment, 90–91
Shays's Rebellion, 28–30
Sherman, Roger, 7, 48, 58
Sixth Amendment, 89–90
slavery, 10–11, 54–60, 94
state conventions, 70, 82–83
strict interpretation of the
   Constitution, 84, 92
Supreme Court, 36, 48, 84, 90

taxation, 11, 16, 20, 22, 26, 27,
   28, 57, 59, 68, 73, 78
Tenth Amendment, 92
Third Amendment, 86–87
Thirteenth Amendment, 57
three-fifths compromise,
   55–56
Treaty of Paris, 24, 25
Twenty-first Amendment, 66

Virginia Bill of Rights, 40
Virginia Plan, 45–47, 48, 66

Washington, George, 21–22,
   30, 31–32, 37, 38–39, 48,
   65, 68, 74, 78
   army career, 7, 9, 21–22
   president of convention,
      43–44, 67
   president of the United
      States, 79–80
   slavery, 58, 59
Williamson, Hugh, 50
Wilson, James, 39, 57, 63–64,
   73

Yorktown, 9, 22, 24

About the Author

Charles Pederson is a writer, editor, and translator. His contributions have appeared in fiction and nonfiction publications for children and adults. He has traveled widely, bringing an appreciation of different peoples and cultures to his work. He lives near Minneapolis, Minnesota, with his wife, two children, a dog, and a cat.

Photo Credits

Lee Pettet/iStockphoto, cover; North Wind Picture Archives, 6, 9, 13, 24, 29, 33, 34, 38, 45, 52, 62, 76, 81, 96, 97 (top); Library of Congress, 14, 61, 82, 98; AP Images, 18, 23, 72, 97 (bottom); Hulton Archive/Stringer/Getty Images, 41; MPI/Stringer/Getty Images, 42; North Wind Picture Archives/Photolibrary, 51, 99 (top); Lee Snider/Photo Images/Corbis, 69; James Steidl/ iStockphoto, 71, 99 (bottom); Jim Mone/AP Images, 85; Ron Edmonds/AP Images, 95